Jellyfish

Jellyfish

Sharon Sharth

THE CHILD'S WORLD®, INC.

Published in the United States of America by The Child's World®, Inc.
PO Box 326
Chanhassen, MN 55317-0326
800-599-READ
www.childsworld.com

Product Manager Mary Berendes
Editor Katherine Stevenson
Designer Mary Berendes
Contributor Bob Temple

Photo Credits
© A. Flowers & L. Newman, The National Audubon Society Collection/Photo Researchers: 29
© 2001 Ben Cropp/www.norbertwu.com: 26
© 2001 Brandon D. Cole: 13
© 2001 Fred Bavendam/Stone: 15
© Jeffrey L. Rotman: 16
© 1999 Kevin Schafer: 30
© 2001 Kevin Schafer/Stone: cover
© 2001 Norbert Wu/www.norbertwu.com: 2, 6, 9, 10, 20, 23, 24
© Robert Hermes, The National Audubon Society Collection/Photo Researchers: 19

Library of Congress Cataloging-in-Publication Data
Sharth, Sharon.
Jellyfish / by Sharon Sharth.
p. cm.
Includes index.
Summary: Describes the physical characteristics, behavior, habitat,
and life cycle of jellyfish.
ISBN 1-56766-613-2 (alk. paper)
1. Jellyfishes—Juvenile literature. [1. Jellyfishes.] I. Title.

QL377.S4 S49 2001
593.5'3—dc21
98-048713

On the cover...

Front cover: These moon jellyfish are feeding in the ocean.
Page 2: The bell of Desmonema glaciale (dez-moh-NEE-muh glay-shee-AL) jellyfish like this one can grow to be over 3 feet across.

Table of Contents

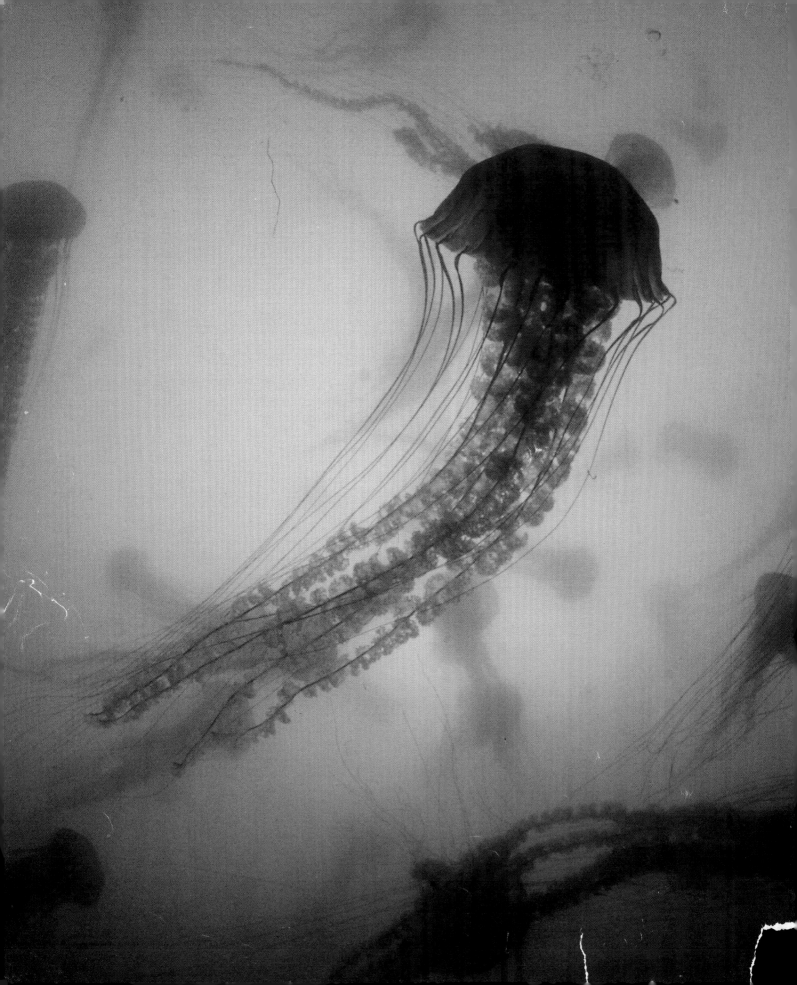

Out in the deep blue sea, an animal moves slowly, pulsing through the water. Its bell-shaped body opens and closes like an umbrella as the animal moves upward. Dangling strings hang from its body like party streamers. What is this strange animal? It's a jellyfish!

⇐ The sea nettles in this large group are floating off the California coast.

What Are Jellyfish?

Jellyfish have been around for 650 million years. In fact, jellyfish are even older than the dinosaurs! Despite their name, jellyfish aren't fish. They are soft, squishy animals that have no bones or shells. Animals that have no bones are called **invertebrates.** Snails, octopuses, and insects are invertebrates, too.

Here a diver is inspecting a giant pelagic (puh-LA-jik) ⇒ jellyfish floating off the coast of California.

Most jellyfish have a body shaped like an umbrella or bell. You can almost see through their bodies! They are made of a jellylike substance that allows them to float. Inside the jelly coating, the jellyfish is hollow. Strings called **tentacles** hang from the main part of the animal's body. These tentacles help the jellyfish catch food. Under the umbrella, the jellyfish has only a huge, open mouth. That is where the jellyfish takes in food and sends out waste products.

⇐ This Desmonema glaciale jellyfish is floating near the ice in Antarctica. Its tentacles can grow to be over 14 feet long.

Are There Different Kinds of Jellyfish?

There are about 200 different kinds, or **species,** of jellyfish. Some are as tiny as a pea. Others, such as *sea blubbers,* can grow to be over six feet across. That's as big as a person! Another large jellyfish is the *lion's mane.* Its clump of tentacles looks like the hair on a lion's head. Lion's mane jellyfish are a brownish purple color.

This lion's mane jellyfish is drifting in the open ocean. ⇒

One of the most common types is the *moon jellyfish.* These animals have smooth, bell-shaped bodies. *Sea nettles* have bell-shaped bodies, too. Sea nettles' tentacles have small stingers on them to kill their food.

Some jellyfish, such as *root-mouthed jellyfish,* have no tentacles. Instead, they have thousands of little mouths for catching their food. Root-mouthed jellyfish are found in warm, tropical waters.

These moon jellyfish are floating near Australia's Ningaloo Reef. ⇒ You can almost see right through them.

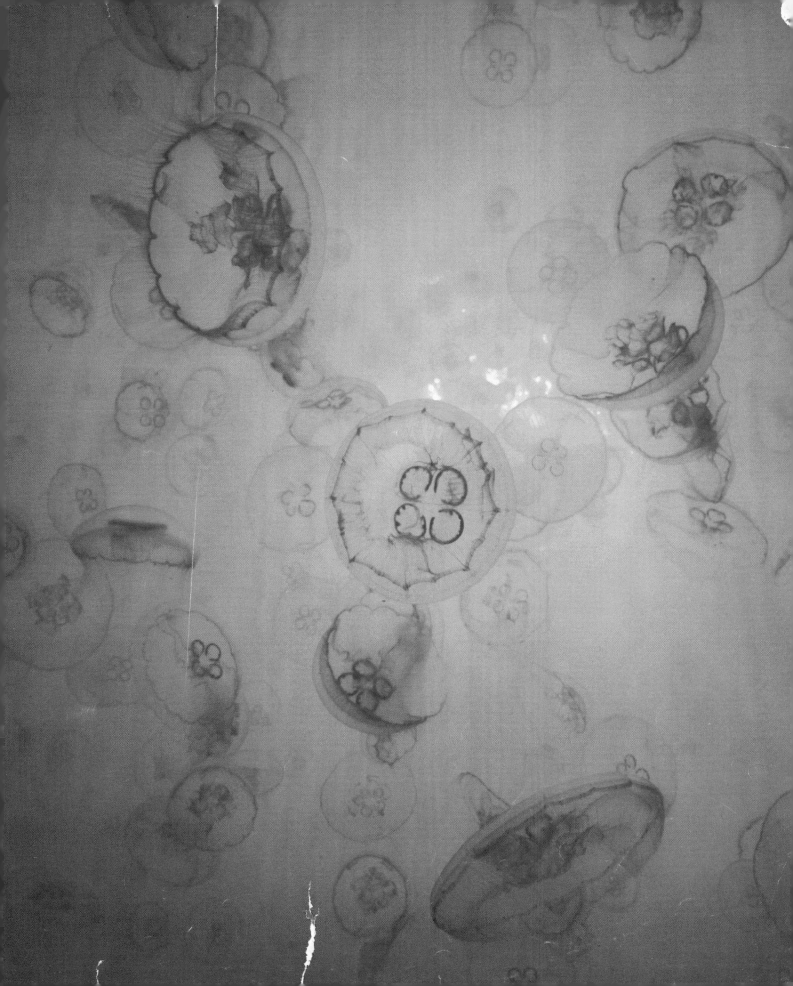

Jellyfish are **carnivores,** which means that they eat other animals. They especially like to eat fish, crabs, and shrimp. They also feast on tiny **zooplankton.** Zooplankton are animals that float along on **currents** of water moving through the sea. Jellyfish are actually zooplankton, too. They often eat other jellyfish!

⇐ The moon jellyfish in this huge cluster are feeding on zooplankton near the ocean's surface.

How Do Jellyfish Catch Their Food?

Like other zooplankton, jellyfish usually float wherever the currents take them. Sometimes, though, they move themselves. They open and close their bodies to push through the water. As a jellyfish moves, its tentacles drag slowly behind. If a fish or other small animal swims by, the tentacles reach out and trap it. Then the jellyfish brings its tentacles up to its mouth and eats its meal.

Different jellyfish have different tricks for catching their food. Some have a sticky gel on their bodies that helps snag passing animals. Others have a strange glow that attracts fish. Some jellyfish have tentacles with stingers that shoot poison into other animals.

This sea nettle has caught a small fish to eat. ⇒

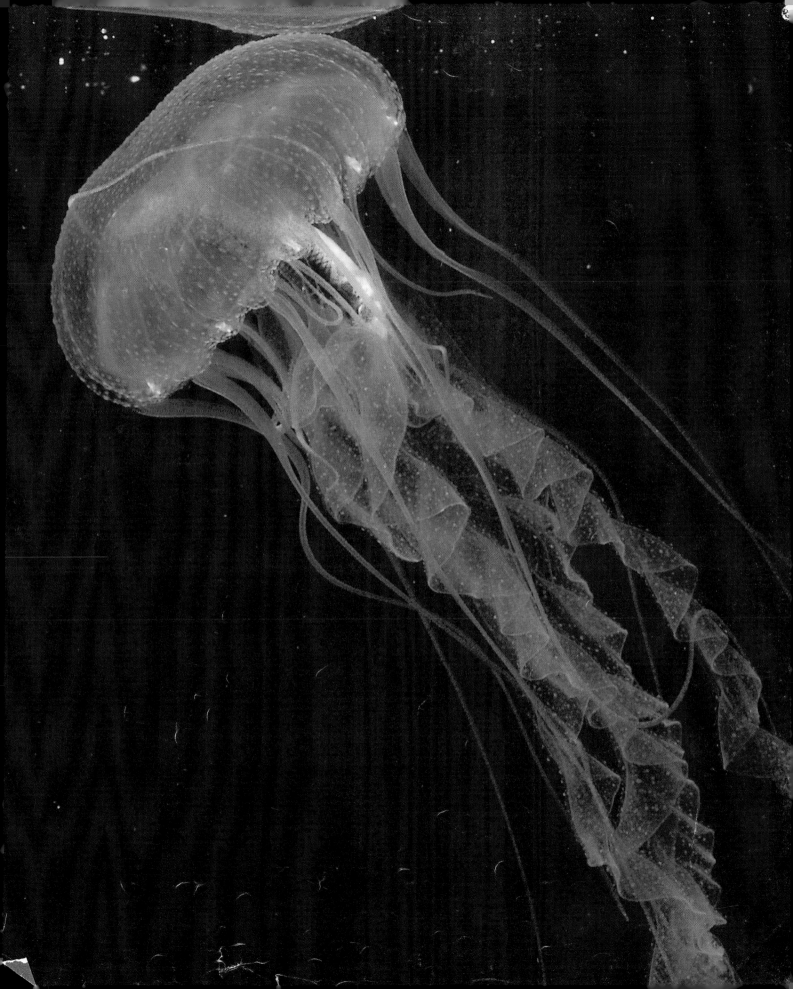

Jellyfish live in all the oceans of the world. Because they drift with the currents, they are found in almost every part of the ocean. They even get blown along by the wind. Often, jellyfish are pushed toward land. There they float near the surface as their tentacles scan for food.

⇐ Portuguese man-of-wars like this one are related to jellyfish. The top part of their bell floats above the water and gets blown by the wind like a boat's sail.

How Are Baby Jellyfish Born?

Adult jellyfish are called **medusas.** When male and female medusas mate, the female releases hundreds of tiny eggs into the sea. The male fertilizes the eggs as they sink to the ocean floor. Soon, each egg grows into a tube-shaped **polyp** that attaches itself to the sea floor. The polyp's mouth and tentacles face upward to find food. The polyp looks like a small hand with many waving fingers.

Later, the polyp divides into what looks like a stack of plates. When the plates get big enough, they pop off and become young jellyfish. These babies grow up to be umbrella-shaped medusas.

This jellyfish polyp is growing in a Borneo lake. ⇒

How Do Jellyfish Protect Themselves?

Like most other animals, jellyfish have enemies. Some kinds of fish, sea turtles, and even birds like to eat jellyfish. Jellyfish can't move fast enough to escape these attackers. Instead, they have other ways of protecting themselves. The easiest way for them to stay safe is to hide! A jellyfish's light or clear color blends in with the water, making the jellyfish harder for enemies to see.

← Here proboscis worms are feeding on a jellyfish that got too close.

Jellyfish also protect themselves with their stinging tentacles. Some jellyfish have poison that can injure or even kill another animal. This poison makes them more dangerous than sharks. *Sea wasps* are one of the most poisonous animals in the world. Their square bodies are only about as big as a shoebox. But a sting from their tentacles can kill a person within three minutes!

How Can We Learn About Jellyfish?

A jellyfish's body is almost all water. If it gets washed ashore, it soon shrivels up and disappears. To get a close look at a jellyfish, look on an ocean beach just after a storm or when the water is low. If you find a jellyfish, remember not to touch it! Even if the jellyfish is dead, its stinging tentacles can hurt you.

This blue bottle jellyfish has washed up on a beach. ⇒

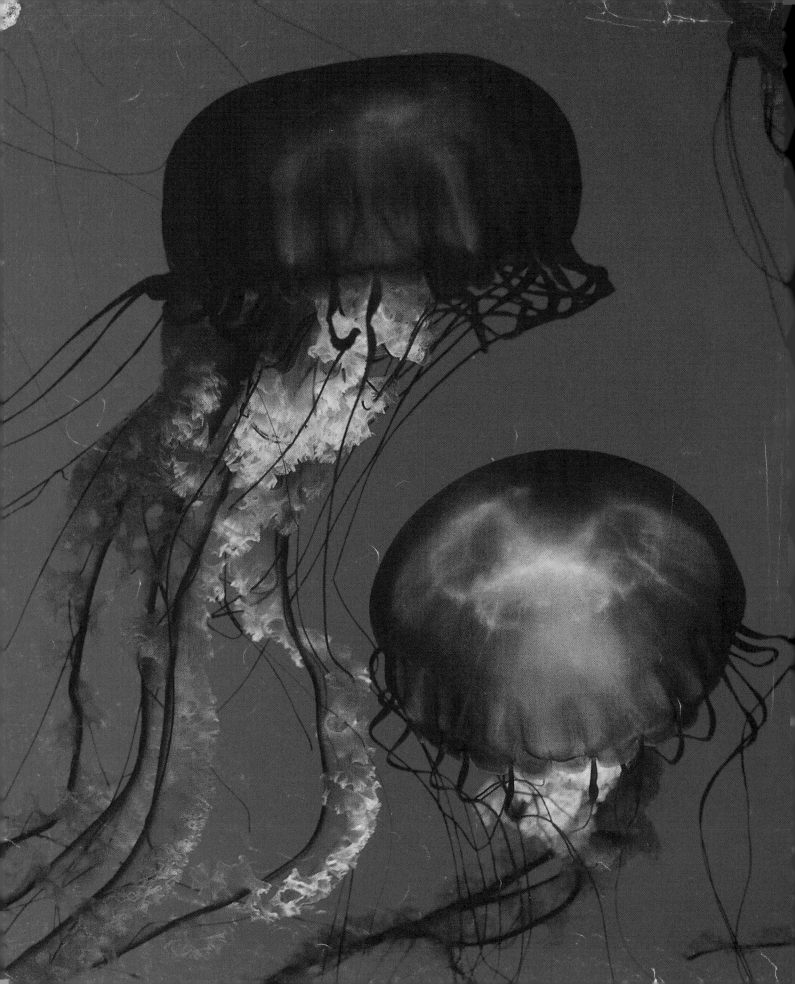

If you go boating on the ocean, keep an eye out for jellyfish. You probably won't want to go swimming with them, but you can have fun watching them float. Zoos and aquariums are good places to see jellyfish, too. Watch how they open and shut their bodies to move around. Count their tentacles. Then think about how far the jellyfish have traveled in their lives. Will you ever see as many places as the jellyfish?

⇐ These sea nettles are floating in a California aquarium.

Glossary

carnivores (KAR-nih-vorz)
Carnivores are animals that eat other animals. Jellyfish are carnivores.

currents (KUR-rentz)
Currents are streams of water that flow within the ocean. The currents carry jellyfish and other floating animals.

invertebrates (in-VER-teh-brets)
Invertebrates are animals that have no skeletons or bones inside their bodies. Jellyfish are invertebrates.

medusas (meh-DOO-suz)
Adult jellyfish are called medusas. The name comes from the Medusa of Greek myths, who had snakes for hair.

polyp (POL-ip)
A baby jellyfish is called a polyp. Polyps have tubelike bodies and fasten themselves to the ocean floor.

species (SPEE-sheez)
A species is a different type or kind of an animal. There are about 200 different species of jellyfish.

tentacles (TEN-teh-kullz)
Tentacles are the moving, armlike strings that hang from a jellyfish's body. The tentacles trap food and bring it to the jellyfish's mouth.

zooplankton (zoh-uh-PLANGK-tun)
Zooplankton are animals that drift along in the water. Jellyfish are zooplankton, and they eat other zooplankton, too.

Index

Web Sites

http://www.aqua.org/animals/species/jellies.html

http://www.aquarium.org/jellies/index.htm

http://www.tennis.org/Special/jellyspecial.html

http://www.nationalgeographic.com/world/9608/jellyfish/index.html#jellyfish